# YOUR KNOWLEDGE HAS VALUE

AF167936

- We will publish your bachelor's and master's thesis, essays and papers

- Your own eBook and book - sold worldwide in all relevant shops

- Earn money with each sale

Upload your text at www.GRIN.com and publish for free

# Quality Management Systems and Processes. The Case of Barclays

Luxmi Kanth Navaneethan

**Bibliographic information published by the German National Library:**

The German National Library lists this publication in the National Bibliography; detailed bibliographic data are available on the Internet at http://dnb.dnb.de.

ISBN: 9783346160706
This book is also available as an ebook.

Print and binding: Books on Demand GmbH, Norderstedt, Germany
Printed on acid-free paper from responsible sources.

The present work has been carefully prepared. Nevertheless, authors and publishers do not incur liability for the correctness of information, notes, links and advice as well as any printing errors.

GRIN web shop: https://www.grin.com/document/538262

# Quality Management Systems and Processes – the Case of "Barclays Group"

Luxmi Kanth Navaneethan

Arden University, Berlin – 25.05.2019

# Table of Contents

# Table of figures

# 1 Task 1

## 1.1 Background

With the increasing demands of customers such a need for better products and services, the current global market has been highly competitive. The source of high products and priced services from small labor costs is increasing for most markets. With the current market competitive threats, improved and results-oriented strategies are essential for organizations and businesses (Chun Hung Cheng, 2012).

It is the customers that are the vital element of all companies and organizations. In most cases, the sales of companies and organizations are determined by customers based on their observation of service quality plus products (Henrik Eriksson, 2010).

Quality tools contribute to improving product, service and process quality. A quality tool is designed in accordance with a defined procedure in order to perform a specific task. It enables improvements and changes to be directed and supported. Two groups can be divided into quality tools: conventional tools and additional instruments. Traditional instruments include the Pareto chart and Ishikawa scheme, which were developed in Japan. The additional tools are less used or are used to solve a problem (Nigel Slack, 2010).

## 1.2 Quality Tools and Techniques

Majority of large establishments use quality tools for different quality control and quality assurance purposes. Though there are decent amount of specific quality tools available for some fields, arenas and practices, some of the quality tools can be used across such areas. These tools of quality remain very general further can be applied in any situation or condition.

In organizations, basic seven quality tools are used. These quality tools can deliver a great deal of information about organizational problems that will help to derive solutions for the same (Juan José Tarí, 2014).

### 1.2.1 Seven Quality Control Tools

Numerical method and graphic method are important points, charts are significant when analyzing problems. Seven quality tools is also called as Q7 , Some individuals say that control chart also is one of the diagrams and stratified sampling is one of the important seven quality control tools (Tony, 2018).

- **Pareto Chart** : When products suffer from various defects, Pareto charts are used, however the imperfections happen at various frequencies or only several records for many of the deficiencies available and different deficiencies accrue different prices.

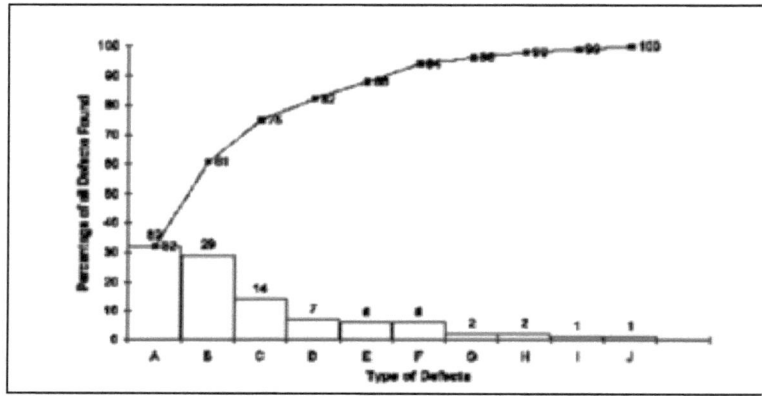

Figure 1: Pareto Chart

- **Histogram** : Graphs of Distribution for 1-dimension data. Histogram is used in two variables to illustrate the frequency and extent. Histogram is chart with columns. This is the mean supply. The chart takes the form of a bell curve if the histogram is usual.

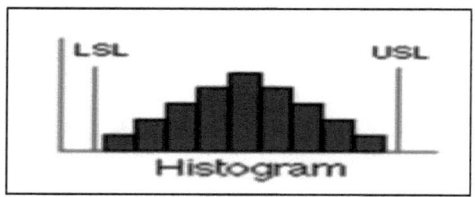

Figure 2 : Histogram

- **Flow Charts**: One of the fundamental quality control tools that can be used to analyze an event sequence. The tool plots a categorization of sequential or parallel occurrences. In order to find the relations and dependences amongst trials, the flow diagram can be used to recognize a multifaceted procedure.

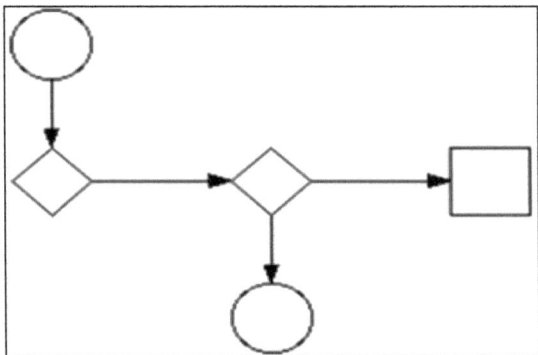

Figure 3 : Flow charts

- **Scatter Diagram** : Graphs with distribution with 2-dimension information. To find the relationship between 2 variables .Scatter diagrams illustrate the positive , negative or neutral relationships between two variables on a plane. Then further analysis can be carried out on the values, such as trend analysis. In these diagrams, one variable refers to one axis and another refers to the other axis.

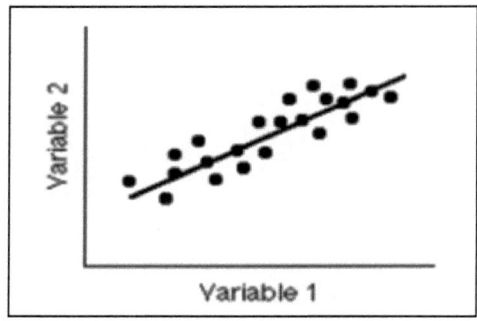

Figure 4: Scatter Diagram

- **Cause & Effect Diagram**: Methodical illustration of cause & effect. Similar like mind mapping. Cause & effect diagrams are used to understand the causes of business or organizational issues.Organizations face problems on a daily basis , to solve them effectively, it is necessary to find the root causes of these problems. Usually exercising the cause & effect diagrams need to done as a team work. For an effective cause & effect diagram, a brainstorming session is required. All the main elements of the area of concern is identified and necessary impacts of each area are mentioned. Then to carry out further analysis , mostly causes of the problems are catergorized nd action plans must be implemented.

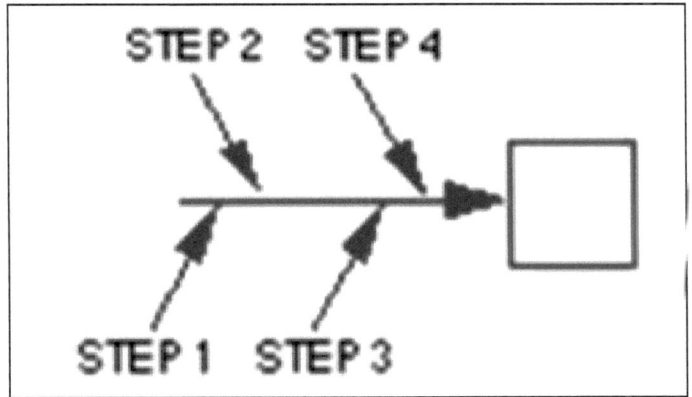

Figure 5 : Cause & effect diagram

- **Check Sheet**: It is possible to introduce a check sheet as the most basic quality control tool. Basically, to collect and organize data, a check sheet is used. Using software programs like MS Excel, it is possible to calculate and optimize even more analysis diagrams using accessible spreadsheets.

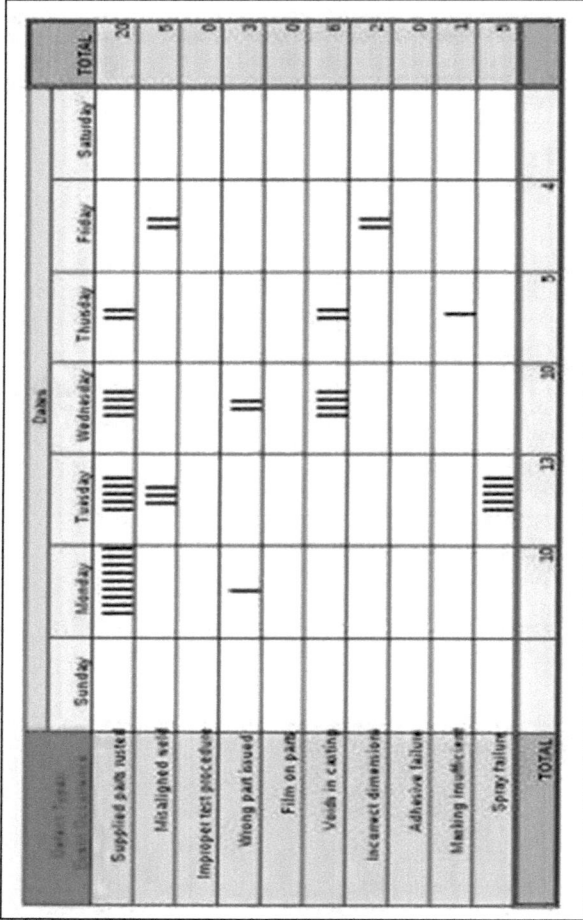

Figure 6 : Check Sheets

- **Control Chart** : Some kind of line graph. It is time for X-dimension. To find the constancy of the movement of information. Control chart is one of the important tools for monitoring and analyzing the process performances. These kinds of control charts can be used for analyzing and monitoring of any procedures connected to function of the company (Tony, 2018).

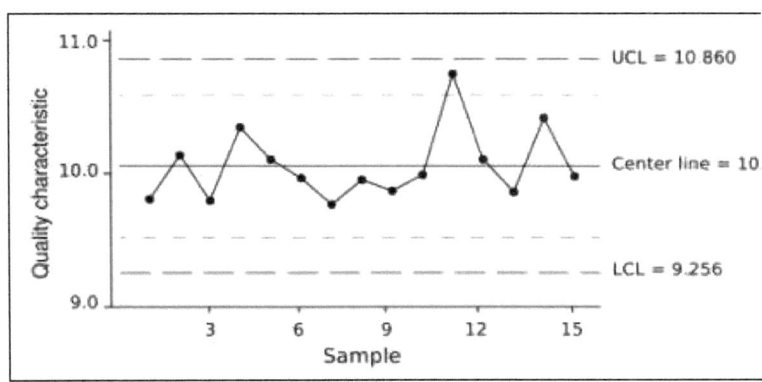

**Figure 7 : Control Charts**

## 1.2.2   New Seven Quality Tools

New seven tools of quality control are made to examine non-quantity data (information) primarily. Those tools could be recognized as cognitive methods. New seven tools of quality is also called N7 (Aichouni, 2018).

- **Affinity Diagram**: An affinity tool is a brainstorming technique that enables teams to break down problems to their component sub-issues, allowing them to isolate the root causes of the problems and provide solutions to them
- **Relation Diagram**: Why-why analysis diagram. It really is useful to use if there is a framework of circulation in the causes and effects
- **Tree Diagram**: Systemically collecting plans and techniques.
- **Matrix Diagram**: A matrix to convey the relationship's strength among two items. Similar like quality function deployment.
- **Process Decision Program Chart**: Similar like flow chart, The Program Chart for Process Decision (PDPC) is a method for helping to plan emergency plans. The PDPC's emphasis is on identifying the significant influence of catastrophe on action plans and developing suitable emergency plans to reduce hazards.
- **Arrow Diagram** : Same like PERT

- **Matrix Data Analysis**: The importance of the matrix statistics analysis diagram is to present and analyze mathematical information in a matrix form about two sets of factors in order to obtain numerical output. Products and product characteristics are the most common factors. The importance is then to analyze the information on multiple features aimed at a sum of products and to use the data to reach at best values for the features of a new item or to determine the strengths of an item and to use the data to design a tactic for product upgrade (Aichouni, 2018).

### 1.2.3 Weakness of Q7 and N7

Applying all seven QC tools for troubleshooting issues within organizations processes is very important. There is no doubt that all the above-mentioned quality tools should be considered and used by management to identify and resolve quality issues during the operations and services.

Most of basic quality tool (Q7) are tools for quantity data examination. But cause & effect diagram and check sheet are for information examination. Most of new quality tools (N7) are tools of knowledge examination. but matrix data analysis is for quantity information examination. And it is mathematically too difficult to study for beginners.

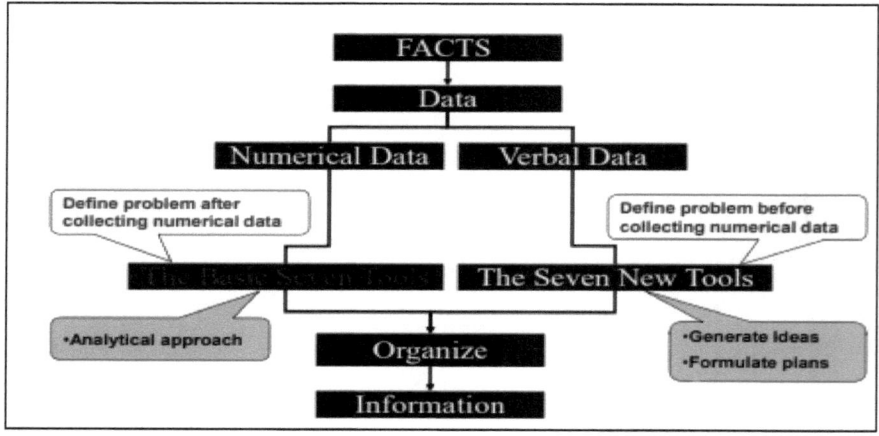

Figure 8 : Relationship Between Q7 & N7

The below figure 9, therefore interprets how to use the 7 QC from first step to end of processes to identify and control quality performance issues.

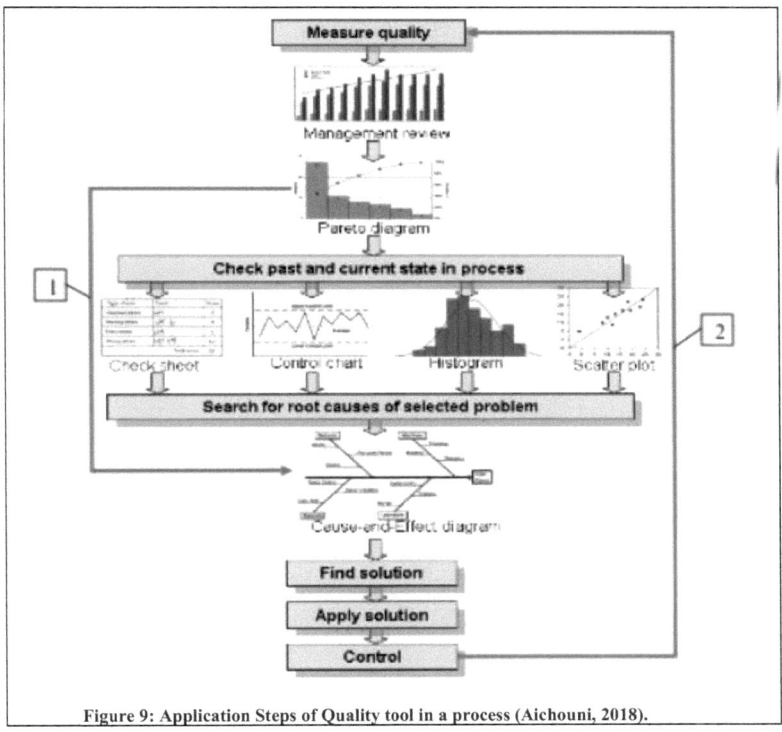

**Figure 9: Application Steps of Quality tool in a process (Aichouni, 2018).**

# 2 Task 2

## 2.1 Solving Customer Related Problems at Barclays Bank

Currently, it is important on the banking market to pay the greatest attention to the customer and to provide exactly the right spectrum of services. Therefore, it is necessary to apply quality management methods and tools to understand their customers and increase their content and loyalty.

Customer focus is a basic principle of modern management that is the basis for virtually all successful business strategies. Maximum customer satisfaction is becoming the prerequisite in order to increase any company's competitiveness.

Banks develop programs to increase the attractiveness of their banking products to attract new customers and maintain their current position. The programs, for example, address the requirements for services of specific groups of customers, develop new banking products and promotional activities, preserve the image of the reliable bank, etc. However, the quality of bank services has more impact on client selection despite the effectiveness of these actions and the fact that banks provide similar types of services.

Improving customer quality leads to greater customer fulfillment, loyalty and repeated purchases. The tools commonly used in quality management initiatives can allow root cause analysis and calculation statistics, process analysis, evaluation of options and customer feedback monitoring. You can learn why quality suffers, learn how to improve processes, reduce waste and enhance customer satisfaction through these tools (Service, 2012).

Cause analytical tools help to understand what went wrong, in addition we can recognize many probable causes for quality problems by drawing a fish bone diagram. This helps to understand why there are problems. Focusing on the most significant problems when investigating the rate of recurrence of problems using a diagram of the Pareto chart. This type of diagram shows the most frequent problems. Concentrate on quality improvements (Service, 2012).

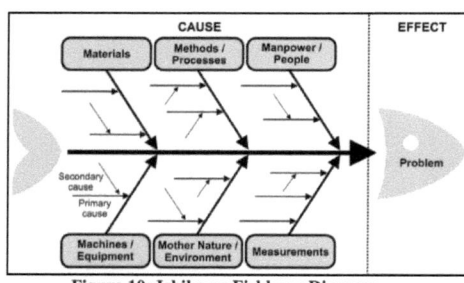
**Figure 10: Ishikawa Fishbone Diagram**

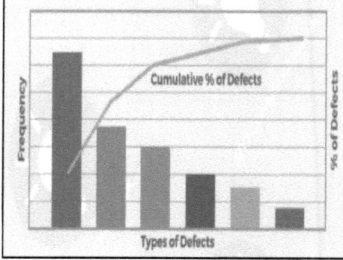
**Figure 11: Pareto Chart**

13

## 2.2    Example 1

In recent past, Barclays customers complained about late payments and difficulties accessing accounts after they blamed Internet and telephone bank breakdowns on a "technical hitch."

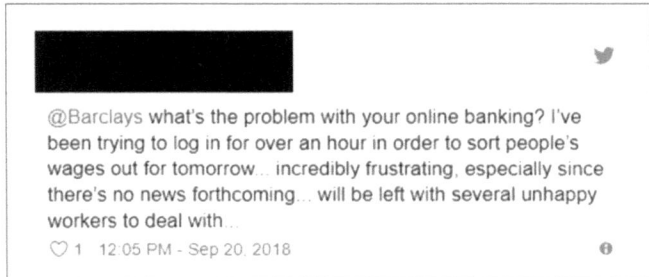

@Barclays what's the problem with your online banking? I've been trying to log in for over an hour in order to sort people's wages out for tomorrow... incredibly frustrating, especially since there's no news forthcoming... will be left with several unhappy workers to deal with...

♡ 1   12:05 PM - Sep 20, 2018

**Figure 12 : Twitter Complaint by Customer**

Many customers have complained that they are not able to organize payments for staff tomorrow while other customers have suggested that they still have problems completing their banking activities following the clear statement by the bank (News, 2018).

In the same day Barclays bank website claimed online and mobile banking have returned to normal.

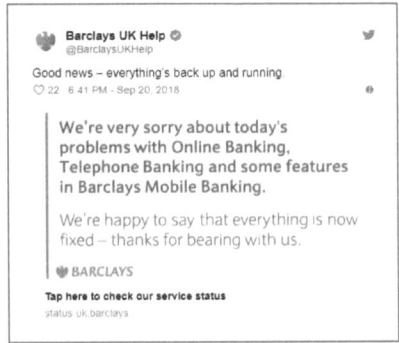

**Figure 13 : Twitter by Barclays Bank**

These kinds of problems can be happening in the future also, so its Barclays responsibility to recognize the root-causes of these problems and make action plans to mitigate them fully. Root cause Analysis will be a great quality management tool in the above situation for Barclays to solve the same problem.

### 2.2.1   Process Analysis

To progress customer quality, companies need to recognize the workflows and process, therefore companies can recognize the inputs, outputs and further details. It aids to separate problems and recognize possible modifications. Then the changes can be measured. Make these changes throughout the company if improvements occur. A decision matrix can also be created to prioritize options. It can be used to assess the choices and make the finest choice by comparing the options with the established criteria.

when product errors lead to customer disappointment, recognize all probable solutions replacements such as replacement, repair or reimbursement of products and later select the finest solution for lower cost and time.

### 2.2.2   Brainstorming

By brainstorming ask a selected set of people and produce ideas about methods to resolve client-quality problems can sort ideas into categories using free concept mapping tools, to give a feedback on a quality issue, for instance, run a focus group with a small group. Make the problem and solution visual map. Later this evidence can be used to develop and improve the quality of customers through product engineering teams.

### 2.2.3   Customer Feedback

The surveys allow companies to gather customer feedback and calculate customer satisfaction. Surveys can be created after customers bought products or services. Get product feedback, problems and needs. Feedbacks can be useful to identify clients with the highest potential to respond to campaigns using this information. By anticipating customer loyalty with preferred treatment rather than waste time for users who do not generate revenue for the company. Improved customer quality means more recommendations, higher incomes and long-lasting achievement.

## 2.3   Example 2

The Barclays bank holds private customers and cooperates with high. The Bank's management has integrated long-term strategies into its processes and services to make sure to create a remarkable customer demand and product and service support. These strategies are always designed to enjoy and surprise their esteemed customers before their competing archers. Not just ensures that esteemed clients buy their products, the management of the Barclay Bank also recommends the products to their friends and families.

An independent survey was carried, to ask customers of the major banking service providers if they will recommend their banks to family and friends. below are the results.

Figure 14 : Quality Scores (GfK, 2019)

### 2.3.1   Online Banking Service

By looking at the score it is evident that Barclays bank have a good service for its online and mobile banking clients, the bank got latest technology such as ATM facilities which saves clients time and thus facilitates their dealings through the bank.

In addition to ATM, the bank used different plans for key products and services to be processed in a lesser time, like new accounts, credit card loans and check encashment. The waiting period, down-time and queuing time have been significantly reduced by innovation in mobile applications.

### 2.3.2   Services in Branches

Even though qualified employees offered banking services improve customer satisfaction, staff are trained to provide friendly and efficient services to customers. The employed times of the bank were estimated appropriate for their clients and staffs on a parallel basis, still Barclays bank ranked 9th for its services in branches. This shows the bank need to improve its weakest service branches to satisfy the customers.

It is recommended that the bank expand its performance as regards service, quality, value and cleanliness rather than limiting its functions in order to make sure the total implementation of management in quality is effective.

### 2.3.3 Overall Service Quality

In comparison with its competitors the bank ranked in the 5th position, by enhancing uses precision and appropriateness of the account reports can guarantee the clients ' confidence in the bank while maintaining the reputation and truthfulness of the bank. These quality improvements can make the Barclays banks to move up in the rank.

### 2.3.4 Conclusion

Consistency is the goal of excellent quality management when providing services, making products, and accomplishing results. It is achieved by applying consistently the techniques and tools related with quality planning, quality assurance and quality control processes. An efficient project manager must also have an outstanding knowledge of work with both the quality tools and methods and therefore should aim for process improvement of the associated processes. Only then will the work truly satisfy the customer.

# 3 References

Aichouni, M., 2018. *The 7 Management and Planning Tool – The 7 New Quality Tools,* Saudi Arabia: Engineering College, Hail University.

Chun Hung Cheng, M. S. M. J. M., 2012. IMPLEMENTING QUALITY MANAGEMENT (QM) IN THE BANKING SERVICES SECTOR. *Total Quality Management,* 7(4), pp. 347-356.

GfK, 2019. *Personal banking service quality – Great Britain.* [Online]
Available at: https://insights.gfk.com/personal-banking-service-quality-great-britain-0
[Accessed 24 05 2019].

Henrik Eriksson, J. T., 2010. The impact of TQM on financial performance. *Measuring Business Excellence,* 7(1), pp. 36-50.

Juan José Tarí, V. S., 2014. Quality tools and techniques: Are they necessary for quality management?. *International Journal of Production Economics,* 92(3), pp. 267-280.

News, S., 2018. *Sky News.* [Online]
Available at: https://news.sky.com/story/barclays-online-banking-goes-down-after-technical-problems-11503039
[Accessed 25 05 2019].

Nigel Slack, S. C. ,. R. J., 2010. *Operations Management.* 6th ed. Pitman Publishing imprint: Essex.

Service, W. S. D. o. E., 2012. *Root Cause Analysis.* [Online]
Available at: https://des.wa.gov/services/risk-management/about-risk-management/enterprise-risk-management/root-cause-analysis
[Accessed 25 05 2019].

Tony, 2018. *7 Tools for Continuous Quality Improvement.* [Online]
Available at: https://toughnickel.com/business/Continuous-quality-Improvement-Quality-Tools
[Accessed 26 05 2019].